THE DEVIL'S HORSE

EMBRACE THE DARKNESS WITHIN, WHERE EMOTIONS RUN DEEP AND WILD.

ADARSH RAI

Made with ♥ on the Notion Press Platform
www.notionpress.com

To my friends, family, and the unknown,

This book is a heartfelt dedication to you - my constant source of support and inspiration. Your unique experiences, stories, and struggles have played a pivotal role in shaping my journey as a writer and have given me the courage to delve deep into the complexities of human emotions. Without your unwavering presence and guidance, this book would not have been possible, and for that, I am forever grateful.

I would like to express my heartfelt appreciation to my friends and family for their constant love, encouragement, and unwavering support. Even when I doubted myself, you have been there to believe in me and provide the foundation for my creative endeavors. Your support has been an integral part of my journey, and I am truly grateful for all that you have done.

To the unknown souls whose experiences have left a profound impact on my being, I offer my heartfelt gratitude. Your courage in sharing your stories, your vulnerability, and authenticity have touched my soul and set my imagination ablaze. You have reminded me of the immense power of storytelling and the incredible importance of empathy in our lives. Though we may never cross paths, your journey has left an indelible mark on mine, and for that, I am eternally grateful.

I hope this book will serve as a testament to the immeasurable gratitude and love I have for all of you - my friends and family. Your presence and impact on my life, as well as my writing journey, have been invaluable. I am humbled and honored to be able to share this work with you, as it is a reflection of the deep appreciation and love I have for each and every one of you.

With love and gratitude!

Contents

Contents

Foreword

The Devil's Horse is a collection of 20 poignant poems that explore the depths of human emotions and relationships. Each piece in this collection is a testament to the author's keen understanding of the complexities of love, loss, and redemption.

Adarsh Rai has a remarkable ability to delve into the nuances of human feeling and express them in vivid and evocative language. His writing is both haunting and beautiful, drawing the reader in and inviting them to explore the dark corners of their own hearts.

In this collection, you will find poems that touch on a range of topics, from the pain of heartbreak to the exhilaration of new love, from the complexities of family relationships to the search for meaning in life. Each piece is a journey in itself, a glimpse into the inner workings of the human soul.

I have had the privilege of reading Adarsh's work over the years and have been consistently impressed by his talent and dedication to his craft. His writing is a reflection of his deep understanding of the human condition and his commitment to exploring it through his art.

I hope that this collection will resonate with readers as deeply as it has with me. May it inspire you to explore the depths of your own emotions and relationships, and to find solace and meaning in the beauty of the written word.

Sincerely,

Parikshit Khanna (Author - Digital Black: The Starting)

Preface

The Devil's Horse is not just a mere collection of poems but rather an invitation to embark on a journey through the intricate and shadowy territories of human emotions. Each piece in this work of art is an immersive experience that offers readers a glimpse into their own deepest fears, longings, and vulnerabilities.

Through the art of poetry, I tried to create a world that enthralls and mesmerizes, stirring something deep within the reader's soul. The Devil's Horse beckons you to explore the depths of your being and discover the truths that lie hidden within.

I have always been fascinated by the intricacies of human emotion and the power of language to capture those emotions. The Devil's Horse is a culmination of my own experiences, observations, and reflections on the human condition.

Through this collection, I hope to offer readers a glimpse into the complexities of our emotions, the depths of our desires, and the fragility of our hearts. I believe that poetry has the power to transcend language and culture, to speak to the deepest parts of our being, and to connect us with one another in profound ways.

It is my hope that this collection will resonate with readers and offer them a space to explore their own emotions and experiences. I am honored to share this work with you and am grateful for the opportunity to offer a window into the human soul through the power of poetry.

1. I long for you, but you are distant to me!

I long for you, but you are distant to me!
I long for you, but you are distant to me
Shifted to bright sky and rocky shore.
Before my eye grew bright and white,
To the soft air, the soft waters play,
Look into my azure heart, and see her smile
Came the soft look of English eye;
I long for you, but you are distant to me
Smoothes these green banks with a tender mold.
She loved and loved my life awhile,
All I could do is long for her
Came the fairy sound with flow;
Read thy blue words of waters like a spell,
Riding all day through the distant shade,
Near the soft wood in the soft summer haze,
Lingering and murmur by my side,
Standing alone, yet my thoughts galore
She gazed on it with an many sign.
I long for you, but you are distant to me...

2. Love and hate, two opposing forces

Love and hate, like rain and drought,
Can both be felt, but love's what life's about.
Love and hate, two opposing forces,
In the heart they dwell, with different courses.
One brings joy, the other pain,
In the same heart, they often reign.
Love, a feeling that's warm and bright,
Fills our hearts with its soft light,
A connection so deep and true,
That nothing else can compare to.
Hate, a fire that burns within,
A cold, dark emotion, its poison seeps in,
A feeling that drives us apart,
Ravages the soul and breaks the heart.
Both love and hate are powerful, that's true,
They shape our lives and shape what we do.
But it's up to us, to choose which way,
To let love guide us, or hate lead astray.
So let us cherish love and fight against hate,
For in this world, love is what we need to create,
A future that's bright, a world that's kind,
Where love and peace, in our hearts we find.

3. Trapped in Pain: A Soul's Desolate Path

A soul lost in a desolate world of pain and sorrow wanders in search of peace and happiness, but every road leads back to the darkness of emptiness and grief. The memories of love have faded, leaving only fears and a bleak future in their wake. A heart once filled with laughter now endures an endless cycle of misery and despair.

Lost and dismal, I wander through the dark
A soul consumed by pain, with no spark
Of hope or happiness to guide my way
In this void of sorrow, I cannot stray.
Memories of love now faded away
Leaving me in a desolate array
Of emptiness and grief that won't subside
This pain inside, I cannot hide.
Days feel endless, nights filled with tears
A heart that once danced, now filled with fears
The laughter of yesterday, now a distant sound
In this lost and dismal world, I am bound.
I search for comfort in the unknown
Hoping to find a place to call my own
But every road leads back to this pain
Leaving me in this misery, again and again.

In this darkness, I cannot see the light
The future is bleak, a endless night
Lost and dismal, I continue to roam
In search of peace, far from this pain and woe.

4. Solitude, Lust and ecstasy - The Triad of Desire

Solitude, Lust and ecstasy - The "Triad of Desire"

Where passions run deep, and love takes its toll."

Lust, a fire that ignites the skin,
A thirst for pleasure, a dangerous sin.
Ecstasy, a rush that consumes the soul,
A feeling so intense, it makes us whole.
Solitude, a peaceful emptiness,
A stillness that echoes with tenderness.
It's in these moments, we find ourselves,
And the secrets of our heart, it delves.
Lust, a flame that burns with desire,
A longing so strong, it can't be tamed by fire.
Ecstasy, a symphony of the senses,
A blissful dance, with no pretenses.
Solitude, a haven from the noise,
A place where the mind and heart rejoice.
In these three states, we find release,
And the essence of our very being.
Lust, ecstasy, and solitude, all three,
Are aspects of life, that we must see.

For they shape us, and make us who we are,
In our hearts, they leave their own unique scar.

5. Betrayal by family, a wound that cuts deep

"Betrayal by family, a wound that cuts deep,
But wisdom and love, will help us to rise and keep."
Lies and deception, a tangled web we weave,
When family betrays us, our hearts they grieve.
Words that deceive, and trust that's broken,
A pain that's felt, when love's unspoken.
The hurt that lingers, when lies are revealed,
Can leave us broken, our hearts concealed.
But it's in these moments, that wisdom is born,
And we learn to rise, after being torn.
For though family may betray, with lies untold,
The love that we hold, in our hearts, will never grow old.
And as we heal, from the wounds that cut deep,
We find the strength, to rise from our sleep.
So let us not despair, when deception comes our way,
For in its wake, wisdom will stay.
And with this newfound strength, we'll find hope,
That brighter days, are just beyond the slope.
For in this world, where lies and deception reign,
It's up to us, to find love and wisdom again.
And with hope in our hearts, we'll rise above it all,
For in the end, love will always stand tall.

6. Friendship, love, lust, and betrayal, they all exist

Friendship, a bond that lasts a lifetime,
A trust that grows, with laughter and chime.
A connection so pure, it brings us great joy,
A shelter in life, where we can be who we are, without any ploy.
Love, a feeling that transcends all time,
A bond that unites, and makes everything shine.
A love so deep, it makes the world a better place,
A source of light, in even the darkest of space.
Lust, a hunger that drives us to desire,
A thirst for pleasure, that cannot be quenched by fire.
A hunger so strong, it can cloud our judgment,
A dangerous game, that often leads to lament.
Betrayal, a pain that cuts to the core,
A wound that leaves scars, that time can't restore.
A breach of trust, that shatters the soul,
A darkness that creeps, taking its toll.
Friendship, love, lust, and betrayal, they all exist,
In our lives, they play a part, with twists and turns that persist.
But it's up to us, to find the balance,
And to choose the path, that will bring us the greatest chance.
For in this world, where love and friendship abound,

We must also guard against the forces that bring us down.
And with wisdom and love, as our guide,
We can find the path, that leads us to where happiness resides.

7. Desire and betrayal, a toxic affair

Desire and betrayal, a toxic affair,
Leaves wounds deeper than what the eye can repair.
Desire, a flame that burns bright and strong,
A hunger so fierce, it can last all night long.
A thirst for pleasure, that can never be quenched,
A driving force, that cannot be wrenched.
Betrayal, a pain that cuts to the core,
A wound that leaves scars, that time can't restore.
A breach of trust, that shatters the soul,
A darkness that creeps, taking its toll.
Together, they dance, a dangerous game,
A cycle of longing, and pain and shame.
For as desire grows, it can lead to deceit,
And betrayal follows, with a crushing defeat.
But enough is enough, and the time has come,
To stand tall, and show the world what we've become.
For we will not be broken, by desire and deceit,
We will rise up, and show the world our defeat.
For in the end, it's not desire or betrayal, that will win,
It's the strength within us, that will carry us to the end.
So let the anger fuel us, let it light the way,
For we will not be defeated, not today.

For we are stronger, than desire and betrayal combined,
And with the power within us, we will rise and shine.
So let us embrace our anger, and channel it with pride,
For we will not be defeated, we will not be denied.

8. Lost in thoughts, a journey of the mind!

Lost in thoughts, a journey of the mind,
Where dreams and reality, are intertwined.
A soulful escape, to a world of pure bliss,
Where peace and contentment, we always miss.
Lost in thoughts, with a mind full of cheer,
Dreaming up adventures, that bring us good cheer.
A world of wonder, where skies are always blue,
And unicorns prance, and the grass is always dew.
But as we dance, through fields of make-believe,
We realize that maybe, our feet need a break to leave.
For as the days turn into nights, and the nights into days,
Our mind needs a rest, from this never-ending craze.
And fear creeps in, like a mischievous cat,
Meowing "Wake up!" because our bed is where we're at.
But we wave our hand, and the fear is gone in a flash,
For in our minds, we're on a thrilling, never-ending bash.
So let's keep dreaming, with a smile on our face,
For in our thoughts, is a fun, exciting place.
And who knows what adventures, await us ahead,
Lost in thoughts, with our dreams, we'll never be dead!

9. Enduring Pain - A test of will and might

Enduring pain, a test of will and might,
A journey to strength, through the darkest night.
A battle within, where courage shines bright,
Forging a hero, with every fight.
Enduring pain, a battle within,
Where every step forward, requires great discipline.
A war of the mind, where the heart takes a beating,
And every breath feels like it's barely retreating.
But still we push on, through the stormy weather,
With a determination, that will last forever.
For we are the heroes, of our own story,
With a strength that comes, from facing our own misery.
And though the fear creeps in, like a shadow in the night,
We remind ourselves, that we are not ready to take flight.
For in the end, it's the battles that we've fought,
That shape us and make us, the person we've sought.
So embrace the pain, for it makes us stronger,
And when the battle is won, we'll stand taller.

10. A labyrinth of thoughts & a mystery shrouded

A mystery shrouded, in the depths of my mind,
A labyrinth of thoughts, that I cannot unwind.
In the desolate depths of my mind, where the winds howl wild,
And the world seems harsh, with no solace for miles.
I find myself wandering, in a wilderness of me,
With a heart heavy, and a soul that's not free.
The pop corns I carry, a reminder of youth,
A symbol of joy, in a life full of truth.
But as I savor each crunch, I'm faced with the truth,
That in this wilderness, I am all alone, with no proof.
The joy they bring, is short lived, a mere spark,
And the despair creeps in, with a mournful dark.
For in this solitude, I am but a stranger,
With no one to share, my fears, my anger.
Yet I cling to the pop corns, a glimmer of hope,
In the depths of my mind, where my thoughts often elope.
For even in the darkest hour, there's a way out,
And with every handful, of pop corns, I shout.
So let me wander, in the wilderness of me,

With a bag of pop corns, and a hope that I'll see,
That in this journey, I am not truly alone,
And the wilderness of me, is where I've grown.

11. Embracing the Shadow: A Cult of Pain

In the depths of my soul, where the shadows reign,
I embrace the darkness, and call it my name.
It creeps and it crawls, a part of my being,
A cult of my own, where pain is freeing.
It whispers my secrets, a voice in my mind,
It shields me from light, and keeps me confined.
It's a comfort in chaos, a solace in strife,
A constant companion, in the depths of my life.
I bask in its shadows, I revel in pain,
For in this embrace, I feel no shame.
It's a pact of the broken, a bond of the lost,
A love of the lonely, at whatever the cost.
And though others may fear it, and run from its call,
I welcome the darkness, and let it enthrall.
For in this embrace, I find peace within,
And in the shadow's grasp, I let my soul spin.
So I bask in its embrace, and revel in the night,
A cult of the lonely, with pain as its light.
For the darkness is my home, my solace, my friend,
And in its embrace, my soul will never bend.

12. The Devil's Dilemma

In the shadows I once roamed,
Embracing darkness as my own.
But with the arrival of the light,
I am forced to confront my fright.
For the brilliance burns my eyes,
And I cower in its holy guise.
I once reveled in the night,
But now fear the morning's sight.
The battle rages within my soul,
As I struggle to keep control.
For the light is pure and true,
While the darkness is what I knew.
And yet, I cannot resist,
The allure of its sweet mist.
For it whispers secrets in my ear,
And I find myself succumbing to fear.
So I stand here in this purgatory,
Torn between two worlds, so contrary.
Fighting for my place in this strife,
As the devil fears the light of life.

13. When Love Visits, I Close My Eyes

I close my eyes, when Love visits me,
For fear of feeling, what I cannot be.
A heart that's broken, a soul that's scarred,
From past heartaches, that have left their mark.
I run from Love, for I know its pain,
The joy it brings, with it comes the rain.
A tempest of emotions, that I cannot control,
A whirlwind of feelings, that takes a toll.
Yet still Love comes, with a gentle touch,
A whisper of hope, that means so much.
A promise of joy, that I cannot deny,
A chance at happiness, that makes me sigh.
I close my eyes, to escape its hold,
For fear of falling, and losing my soul.
But still Love comes, with an unrelenting grace,
A beacon of light, that shines on my face.
So I open my eyes, and face my fears,
For Love is a gift, that brings me tears.
With each passing moment, my heart is set free,
By the love that visits, and sets me free.

14. The Paradox of Light and Dark: A Contradictory Conundrum

In the embrace of light, the world is warm and bright,
And shadows fade away, with the morning light.
It shines a path ahead, with a gentle ray,
And lifts our hearts with hope, in a bright display.
But in the depths of night, there's a stillness and peace,
A time to reflect, on the joys and release.
And as the moon rises, with its gentle glow,
The world seems softer, in its ebb and flow.
So which is better, the light or the dark?
Is it the warm embrace, or the stillness in the park?
Perhaps it's neither, for both bring their own,
A time for reflection, and a time for hope's throne.
For just as the day needs the night,
And the night needs the day, so bright.
So embrace the light, and bask in its glow,
But don't forget the peace, of the dark's afterglow.
For in the end, it's the balance we seek,
The perfect harmony, of light and dark, unique.

15. Chained by Deception

I lied and I lied, till my words became my curse,
A web of deceit, that I weaved and I nursed.
With each fib, I spun, I felt my soul grow cold,
And in this world of lies, I became lost and alone.
I thought that I could hide, from the truth I'd concealed,
But my guilt and my fear, began to be revealed.
The weight of my lies, started to take its toll,
And my heart filled with pain, as my lies began to unfold.
I wandered aimlessly, in this world I'd created,
Where truth was a stranger, and my soul was debated.
I searched for a way out, but my path was unclear,
And my lies had trapped me, in this world of despair.
But then a glimmer of hope, shone in the distance,
A ray of light, in the darkness of existence.
And I knew then, that I had to break free,
And find redemption, for the lies that I'd believed.
So I mustered my courage, and faced my fears head on,
And took the first step, towards a new dawn.
For even in this world of lies, I must believe,
That the truth will set me free, and bring me relief.

16. Love's Descent into the Abyss of Night

When the moon is gone and the skies are dark,
Love is quarantined, left with a heart-rending mark.
In the stillness of night, with nothing but silence,
Our hearts are shattered, with no chance for reliance.
No longer do we bask, in the warm glow of love,
No longer do we dance, under the stars above.
For when the moon is absent, love is put to the test,
And all that remains, is an emptiness and unrest.
But just as the moon, rises again with grace,
Love too finds its way, back into its place.
And in the light of the moon, our hearts come alive,
And we bask in the love, that makes us thrive.
So let us not fear, the absence of the moon,
For it is only a moment, that shall be over soon.
For when the moon returns, love will follow suit,
And in its warm embrace, our hearts will feel its soothe.

17. In Search of Serenity: A Journey Through Love, Betrayal, and Deceit

In the depths of my heart, I thought love was real,
A bond unbreakable, a bond I could feel.
But little did I know, that love can be fake,
A disguise for deceit, a heartbreak to make.
I trusted in you, with all that I am,
But you tore my heart apart, with your cold, deceitful hand.
Betrayal and lies, were all that I found,
And now I'm left with wounds, that won't heal or bound.
The pain is immense, and the hurt is deep,
My soul is broken, and I can barely sleep.
For love was my refuge, my solace, my home,
And now I'm lost in the darkness, all alone.
But I won't give up, I won't lose my faith,
For I will find a love, that's true and can stay.
I'll search for a love, that's unbreakable and kind,
A love that will heal, and peace to my mind.
So I'll keep searching, in this world so cruel,
For a love that's pure, and free from deceit and duels.
And when I find it, I'll cherish it with all my might,
For love is the only, true and absolute light.

18. The Mask of Success

In this world of ambition, where success is key,
We wear a mask of triumph, with a smile so neat.
Hiding our failures, and our weaknesses untold,
For in this cutthroat game, only the strong unfold.
We strive for greatness, with a hunger so insane,
And we fight for recognition, through our endless pains.
For in this rat race, there is no room for rest,
And we must keep running, or fall among the less.
But what is success, if it's built on deceit,
With a facade of happiness, and a heart so incomplete.
For in the eyes of others, we are but what we show,
And the mask of success, is all they'll ever know.
So we wear this disguise, with a mask so tight,
And we walk with pride, with our heads held high.
But in the quiet of night, when the mask comes off,
We are left with nothing, but our own private cost.
So here's to the game, where we all pretend,
And the mask of success, that will never end.
For in this world of corporate, where only the strong survive,
We are but players, in this endless drive.

19. A Whisper in the Wind

In the quiet of the night, when all is still,
I hear a whisper in the wind, a voice so shrill.
A call to love, a call to trust, a call to be mine,
A call from someone unknown, so rare and so fine.
My heart is racing, my thoughts astray,
As I try to capture this voice that's come to stay.
Is it a dream, a fantasy, or is it real?
This love, this charm, this call that I feel.
The wind is blowing, the night is dark,
As I follow the voice, through the park.
Is it a mirage, a fleeting moment in time?
Or is it the start, of a love so divine?
I search and I seek, with eyes wide open,
For the one who calls, with a voice so hopin'.
I long to find, this love that's unknown,
To bask in its beauty, and never be alone.
So I listen to the wind, and follow its trail,
To the source of the voice, that's bound to unveil.
And as I come closer, I feel it within,
This love, this charm, this call, I win.

20. The Silent Scream

The weight of the world, on fragile shoulders so slim,
The expectations high, but the pressure grows grim.
In a world where success is all that is seen,
The mental health of students is often neglected and unseen.
With eyes focused on the prize, they strive every day,
But the fear of failure, takes its toll in a harsh way.
The reality of the corporate world, is a distant dream,
And the reality of the present, is a silent scream.
They pour their hearts out, in hopes of a brighter future,
But the fear of judgment, takes over like a torture.
The pressure to succeed, takes a toll on their mind,
Leaving them lost, in a world so unkind.
Yet they push on, in hopes of a brighter tomorrow,
Hoping that one day, they'll find peace and not just sorrow.
For their struggles are real, and their fears are so strong,
And their mental health, is something that needs to be cherished and not wronged.
So let's be there for them, and lift them up high,
And show them love, in a world where love is denied.
For mental health is a battle, that cannot be won alone,
And together, we can help them find a brighter home.

Message From The Author

The depth and complexity of human emotion are brought to our attention as we near the conclusion of this voyage via The Devil's Horse. Although the hardships and darkness we have discovered are an important aspect of our human experience, they do not make us who we are.

There is always a glimmer of hope, a ray of light that serves as a reminder of the magnificence and tenacity of the human spirit, even in the midst of suffering and tragedy. May these poems motivate you to accept your own frailties and to persevere in the face of difficulty.

Keep in mind that one of the most potent energies in the universe is love, despite it occasionally being difficult and elusive. May the realization that you are not alone bring you comfort.

May this book be a reminder that in the darkest of times, there is still hope, and that the human spirit is capable of enduring and overcoming even the most difficult of trials.

9 798889 868064

Printed by Libri Plureos GmbH in Hamburg,
Germany